TAGINE

Spicy stews from Morocco

TAGINE

Spicy stews from Morocco

RYLAND
PETERS
& SMALL

LONDON NEW YORK

Ghillie Başan

photography by Martin Brigdale

Dedication
For Monica. To shopping in Marrakesh!

Acknowledgements
I would like to thank the team at Ryland Peters & Small:
Alison Starling, for inviting me to write this book, and Liz
Sephton and Ann Baggaley for whipping it into shape.
And I am thrilled that the ever-so-skilled Martin Brigdale
took the photographs and, as always, made each one look
stunningly appetizing.

First published in Great Britain in 2007
by Ryland Peters & Small
20–21 Jockey's Fields
London WC1R 4BW
www.rylandpeters.com

20 19 18 17 16 15 14

Text © Ghillie Başan 2007
Design and photographs
© Ryland Peters & Small 2007

Printed in China

For digital editions visit
www.rylandpeters.com/apps.php

ISBN 978 1 84597 478 7

A CIP record for this book is available
from the British Library.

Designer Liz Sephton
Editor Ann Baggaley
Production Gemma Moules
Publishing Director Alison Starling

Food Stylists Bridget Sargeson, Lucy McKelvie
Assistant Food Stylist Stella Sargeson
Stylist Helen Trent
Assistant Stylist Isolde Summerscale
Assistant Photographer Nat Davies
Indexer Hilary Bird

Note
All spoon measurements are level unless otherwise stated.

contents

The Secret of Tagines

The classic dish from the region of North Africa known as the Maghreb – Morocco, Tunisia and Algeria – a tagine is a glorified stew worthy of poetry. Aromatic and syrupy, zesty and spicy, or sweet and fragrant are just some of the words that come to mind. A dish of tender meat or succulent vegetables, simmered to perfection in buttery sauces with fruit, herbs, honey and chillies, an authentic tagine is in a class of its own and has become a fundamental feature of Moroccan cuisine.

The name 'tagine' (sometimes spelled 'tajine') is also given to the vessel in which the food is cooked: a shallow, round, earthenware pot with a unique conical lid designed to lock in moisture and flavours, cooking the food gently in a small amount of liquid. The finished dish can either be served piping hot straight from its cooking vessel, or tipped into one of the decorative versions of the pot, glazed in beautiful shades of blue and green, to take to the table.

Originally a Berber dish, the tagine has evolved with the history of the region as waves of Arab and Ottoman invaders, Moorish refugees from Andalusia and French colonialists have left their influences on the cuisine. Classic tagines include combinations of lamb with dried prunes or apricots; chicken with preserved lemon and green olives; duck with dates and honey; and fish cooked with tomatoes, lime and coriander. In the modern

Maghreb, the Berbers are still renowned for their tasty, pungent tagines made with onions and clarified butter.

Traditionally, tagines are served as a course on their own, with freshly baked flat breads or crusty loaves to mop up the delectable syrupy sauces, and are followed by a mound of couscous. The more modern way is to combine the courses and serve them with an accompanying salad. On festive occasions, the custom is to pile up a huge pyramid of couscous and hollow out the peak to form a well into which the tagine is spooned. However, most earthenware tagines are not big enough to cope with feasts, so large copper pots are often used instead.

The great secret of an authentic tagine is to simmer the ingredients over a low heat, so that everything remains deliciously moist and tender. Meat tagines may be cooked for several hours, the meat simmering gently in a seasoned, fragrant liquid until it is so tender it almost falls off the bone. Generally, dishes of vegetables, pulses or fish do not require long cooking times but still benefit from the tagine method in terms of enhanced taste and texture.

Traditionally, tagines are cooked over a clay stove, or brazier, which is stoked with charcoal to maintain constant heat. Such stoves diffuse the heat around the base of the tagine, enabling the liquid to reduce and thicken without drying out. Wood-burning ovens and open fires are used, too. However, wonderful tagines can also be produced using a modern hob or oven.

Most authentic tagines have a little hole at the top of the conical lid to release some of the steam, so that it doesn't try to escape at the seam between the base and the lid. If there is no hole, you will probably need at intervals to tilt the lid at an angle to release the steam yourself. When cooking in an oven, it is generally only the base of the tagine that is used.

There are a number of cooking tagines to choose from, but few of them come with a warning about their vulnerability over a conventional gas hob. Most of the factory-made vessels, whether they are glazed or not, tend to form hairline cracks when they are placed over a gas flame; and they cannot be used on an electric ring. So what do you do? For a glazed earthenware tagine, a heat diffuser is essential, otherwise it is worth splashing out on a durable cast-iron version with a glazed, earthenware lid. A solid, heavy-based casserole pot is a good substitute, as long as you keep the heat very low. But for a tasty, succulent meal, full of flavour and adventure, it is well worth attempting to cook with the genuine article.

TAGINE ESSENTIALS

At the heart of an authentic tagine you will find several traditional ingredients that are indispensable if you want to achieve the delightful balance of hot, spicy, sweet and tart. Most of these ingredients can be found in specialist stores, but it is well worth trying to make some of them at home.

preserved lemons

10 organic, unwaxed lemons
about 10 tablespoons sea salt
freshly squeezed juice of
   3–4 lemons

MAKES 1 LARGE JAR

Added to many dishes as a refreshing, tangy ingredient or garnish, preserved lemons are essential to the cooking of tagines. You can buy jars of ready-preserved lemons in Middle Eastern and African stores, as well as some supermarkets, but it is better to make your own. Be as liberal as you like, tossing them in salads and scattering them over your favourite tagines.

Wash and dry the lemons and slice the ends off each one. Stand each lemon on one end and make two vertical cuts three-quarters of the way through it, as if cutting it into quarters but keeping the base intact. Stuff 1 tablespoon of salt into each lemon, then pack them into a large jar (which has been sterilized by immersion in boiling water and left to drain). Store in a cool place for 3–4 days to soften the lemon skins.

To complete the process, press the lemons down into the jar, so they are even more tightly packed. Pour the freshly squeezed lemon juice over the salted lemons, until they are completely covered. Seal the jar and store it in a cool place for at least 1 month. Rinse the salt off the preserved lemons before using.

harissa

This fiery paste is popular throughout North Africa, served as a condiment or as a dip, or stirred into tagines and couscous to emit its distinct chilli taste. This recipe is for the basic paste, to which other ingredients such as fennel, coriander and mint can be added. Ready-prepared harissa is available in African and Middle Eastern stores, and some supermarkets and delicatessens.

8 dried red chillies (Horn or New Mexico), deseeded
2–3 garlic cloves, chopped
½ teaspoon sea salt
1 teaspoon ground cumin
1 teaspoon ground coriander
4 tablespoons olive oil

MAKES APPROXIMATELY 4 TABLESPOONS
(a little harissa goes a long way)

Put the chillies in a bowl and pour over enough warm water to cover them. Leave them to soak for 1 hour. Drain and squeeze out any excess water. Using a mortar and pestle, pound them to a paste with the garlic and salt (or whizz them in a food processor). Beat in the cumin and coriander and bind with the olive oil.

Store the paste in a sealed jar in the refrigerator with a thin layer of olive oil floating on top. It will keep well for a month.

ras-el-hanout

There is no one recipe for ras-el-hanout, a lovely pungent spice mix, packed with strong Indian aromas of cinnamon, cloves and ginger combined with local African roots and the delicate, perfumed notes of rosebuds. Every family has its own favourite blend. Some of the spices are available only in the Maghreb, so if your tagine recipe calls for this flavouring your easiest solution is to select one of the ready-prepared spice mixes available in Middle Eastern and African stores. You can also order a moist, aromatic ras-el-hanout online from the spice specialists Seasoned Pioneers at www.seasonedpioneers.co.uk.

ghee

Ghee (generally known as *samneh* or *samna* in the Arab world), is clarified and evaporated butter. It is sold in cans in Indian, North African and Middle Eastern shops, as well as in some delicatessens.

To make ghee, simply melt some butter in a heavy-based pan and simmer it until all the water has evaporated, leaving a clear fat with a nutty aroma and taste.

In Morocco, a more pungent clarified butter, *smen*, is made by leaving ghee to mature for several weeks in earthenware pots.

TRADITIONAL LAMB TAGINES

In Arab culture, dates are an age-old source of nutrition and natural sugar; nomads could survive in the desert with dates alone for nourishment. As the fruit is regarded as special, it is often added to festive grain dishes and stews. This slightly sticky date and nut tagine is a favourite at weddings or other family feasts.

lamb tagine with dates, almonds and pistachios

2–3 tablespoons ghee (see page 9) (or olive oil, plus a knob of butter)
2 onions, finely chopped
1–2 teaspoons ground turmeric
1 teaspoon ground ginger
2 teaspoons ground cinnamon
1 kg lean lamb, from the shoulder, neck or leg, cut into bite-sized pieces
250 g moist, ready-to-eat, stoned dates
1 tablespoon dark, runny honey
sea salt and freshly ground black pepper
1 tablespoon olive oil
a knob of butter
2–3 tablespoons blanched almonds
2 tablespoons shelled pistachios
a small bunch of fresh flat leaf parsley, finely chopped

SERVES 4

Heat the ghee in a tagine or heavy-based casserole. Stir in the onions and sauté until golden brown. Stir in the turmeric, ginger and cinnamon. Toss in the meat, making sure it is coated in the spice mixture. Pour in enough water to almost cover the meat and bring it to the boil. Reduce the heat, cover with a lid and simmer gently for roughly 1½ hours.

Add the dates and stir in the honey. Cover with a lid again and simmer for another 30 minutes. Season with salt and lots of black pepper.

Heat the olive oil with the butter in a small pan. Stir in the almonds and pistachios and cook until they begin to turn golden brown. Scatter the nuts over the lamb and dates and sprinkle with the flat leaf parsley. Serve with buttery couscous (see page 60) and a sharp, crunchy salad with preserved lemon (see page 8) to cut the sweetness.

11

This is a lovely winter dish, decorated with ruby-red pomegranate seeds. Whole, meaty chestnuts are often used in Arab-influenced culinary cultures as a substitute for potatoes. You can use freshly roasted nuts or ready-peeled, vacuum-packed or frozen chestnuts.

lamb tagine with chestnuts, saffron and pomegranate seeds

2 tablespoons ghee (see page 9)
2 onions, finely chopped
4 garlic cloves, finely chopped
25 g fresh ginger, peeled and finely chopped or shredded
a pinch of saffron threads
1–2 cinnamon sticks
1 kg lean lamb, from the shoulder or leg, cut into bite-sized pieces
250 g peeled chestnuts
1–2 tablespoons dark, runny honey
sea salt and freshly ground black pepper
seeds of 1 pomegranate, pith removed
a small bunch of fresh mint leaves, chopped
a small bunch of fresh coriander leaves, chopped

SERVES 4

Heat the ghee in a tagine or heavy-based casserole. Stir in the onions, garlic and ginger and sauté until they begin to colour. Add the saffron and cinnamon sticks, and toss in the lamb. Pour in enough water to almost cover the meat and bring it to the boil. Reduce the heat, cover with a lid and simmer gently for about 1 hour.

Add the chestnuts and stir in the honey. Cover with the lid again and cook gently for a further 30 minutes, until the meat is very tender. Season to taste with salt and plenty of black pepper and then toss in some of the pomegranate seeds, mint and coriander. Sprinkle the remaining pomegranate seeds and herbs over the lamb, and serve with bread or a buttery couscous (see page 60).

A classic lamb tagine, sweetened with honey and fruit, is a perfect introduction to the tastes of Morocco. Traditionally, this aromatic dish is served with bread to mop up the syrupy sauce. To balance the sweetness, you could also serve a crunchy salad of finely shredded carrot, onions and cabbage or peppers, spiked with chilli.

lamb tagine with prunes, apricots and honey

1–2 tablespoons olive oil
2 tablespoons blanched almonds
2 red onions, finely chopped
2–3 garlic cloves, finely chopped
a thumb-sized piece of fresh ginger, peeled and chopped
a pinch of saffron threads
2 cinnamon sticks
1–2 teaspoons coriander seeds, crushed
500 g boned lamb, from the shoulder, leg or shanks, trimmed and cubed
about 12 stoned prunes, soaked for 1 hour and drained
about 6 dried apricots, soaked for 1 hour and drained
3–4 strips unwaxed orange zest
1–2 tablespoons dark, runny honey
sea salt and freshly ground black pepper
a handful of fresh coriander leaves, finely chopped

SERVES 4–6

Heat the oil in a tagine or heavy-based casserole, stir in the almonds and cook until they turn golden. Add the onions and garlic and sauté until they begin to colour. Stir in the ginger, saffron, cinnamon sticks and coriander seeds. Toss in the lamb, making sure it is coated in the onion and spices, and sauté for 1–2 minutes.

Pour in enough water to just cover the meat and bring it to the boil. Reduce the heat, cover the tagine or casserole and simmer for about 1 hour, until the meat is tender. Add the prunes, apricots and orange zest, cover the tagine again, and simmer for a further 15–20 minutes. Stir in the honey, season with salt and pepper to taste, cover and simmer for a further 10 minutes. Make sure there is enough liquid in the pot, as you want the sauce to be syrupy and slightly caramelized, but not dry.

Stir in some of the fresh coriander and reserve the rest to sprinkle over the top of the dish. Serve immediately with chunks of crusty bread or buttery couscous (see page 60).

Originally from Andalusia, tfaia tagines are popular in northern Morocco, particularly in Tangier. Their trademark is a pungent, nutty flavour that emanates from matured, clarified butter called *smen* – which is an acquired taste for some people. In this recipe, I use ghee, which is ordinary clarified butter.

tfaia tagine with onions, browned almonds and eggs

1–2 tablespoons ghee (see page 9)
2 garlic cloves, crushed
1 teaspoon ground ginger
1 teaspoon ground coriander
1 teaspoon saffron threads, ground
 with salt
1 kg lamb cutlets
2 onions, finely chopped
175 g brown Kalamata olives, stoned
2 preserved lemons (see page 8),
 cut into quarters
sea salt and freshly ground black pepper
a small bunch of fresh coriander,
 chopped

TO SERVE:
4 medium or large eggs
½ teaspoon ground saffron, or a pinch of
 saffron threads
½ tablespoon ghee
2 tablespoons blanched almonds

SERVES 4

Melt the ghee in a tagine or heavy-based casserole. Stir in the garlic, ginger, ground coriander and saffron, and roll the lamb cutlets in the mixture. Sprinkle the onions over the cutlets and pour in just enough water to cover the meat. Bring the water to the boil, reduce the heat, cover with a lid and cook gently for about 1½ hours.

Add the olives and lemon quarters and cook, uncovered, for about another 20 minutes to reduce the sauce. Season well with salt and black pepper and toss in the chopped coriander.

Meanwhile, boil the eggs in their shells for about 4 minutes, so that the yolk is just firm, and shell them. Dissolve the saffron in 2 tablespoons warm water and roll the eggs in the yellow liquid to colour them. Cut the eggs in half lengthways.

In a frying pan, melt the ghee and stir in the almonds until golden brown. Sprinkle the almonds over the tagine and arrange the eggs around the edge. Serve immediately with fresh, crusty bread and a leafy salad.

Summer tagines using seasonal vegetables are often quite light and colourful. Other vegetables that might be added to this tagine include tomatoes, aubergines and peas. This dish is particularly good served with wedges of lemon to squeeze over it, or with finely shredded preserved lemon (see page 8) sprinkled over the top.

summer tagine of lamb, courgettes, peppers and mint

3–4 tablespoons olive oil
1 onion, roughly chopped
4 garlic cloves, roughly chopped
1 teaspoon cumin seeds
1 teaspoon coriander seeds
1 teaspoon dried mint
25 g fresh ginger, peeled and finely chopped or grated
750 g lean lamb, cut into bite-sized pieces
sea salt and freshly ground black pepper
2 small courgettes, sliced thickly on the diagonal
1 red or green pepper, deseeded and cut into thick strips
4 tomatoes, skinned, deseeded and cut into chunks
a small bunch of fresh flat leaf parsley, roughly chopped
a small bunch of fresh mint leaves, roughly chopped
1 lemon, cut into quarters, to serve

SERVES 4–6

Heat the olive oil in a tagine or heavy-based casserole. Stir in the onion, garlic, cumin and coriander seeds, dried mint and ginger. Once the onions begin to soften, toss in the meat and pour in enough water to just cover it. Bring the water to the boil, reduce the heat, cover with a lid and cook gently for about 1½ hours.

Season the cooking juices with salt and pepper. Add the courgettes, pepper and tomatoes, tucking them around the meat (add a little more water if necessary). Cover with a lid again and cook for about 15 minutes, until the courgettes and pepper are cooked but retain a bite.

Toss in some of the chopped parsley and fresh mint, sprinkle the rest over the top and serve immediately with lemon wedges to squeeze over the dish.

This summery tagine is best accompanied by a fresh green salad of young beet, spinach and lettuce leaves.

In this festive dish, a shoulder of lamb is marinated in chermoula –
a Moroccan herb and spice mix – and baked slowly. You can use
apples or pears instead of quinces. Buttery couscous (see page 60)
or roasted potatoes and a leafy salad are good accompaniments.

baked tagine of lamb with quinces, figs and honey

1.5 kg shoulder of lamb on the bone
2 tablespoons ghee (see page 9)
2 red onions, cut into wedges
225 g ready-to-eat prunes, stoned
225 g ready-to-eat dried figs, or fresh
  figs, halved
40 g butter
2 fresh quinces, quartered and cored
  (keep soaked in water with a squeeze
  of lemon until ready to use)
2–3 tablespoons orange flower water
2 tablespoons dark, runny honey
a bunch of fresh flat leaf parsley,
  chopped
a bunch of fresh coriander, chopped
FOR THE CHERMOULA:
4 garlic cloves, chopped
40 g fresh ginger, peeled and chopped
1 red chilli, deseeded and chopped
1 teaspoon sea salt
a small bunch of fresh coriander, chopped
a small bunch of fresh flat leaf parsley,
  chopped
2–3 teaspoons ground coriander
2–3 teaspoons ground cumin
3 tablespoons olive oil
2 tablespoons dark, runny honey
freshly squeezed juice of 1 lemon

SERVES 4–6

First, make the chermoula. Using a mortar and pestle, pound the garlic, ginger, chilli and salt to form a coarse paste. Add the fresh coriander and parsley and pound into the paste. Beat in the ground coriander and cumin, and bind with the olive oil, honey and lemon juice (alternatively, you can whizz all the ingredients in an electric blender). Cut small incisions in the shoulder of lamb with a sharp knife and rub the chermoula well into the meat. Cover and leave in the refrigerator for at least 6 hours, or overnight.

Preheat the oven to 180°C (350°F) Gas 4.

Heat the ghee in a tagine or heavy-based casserole, add the lamb and brown it all over. Transfer the meat to a plate. Stir the onions and any leftover chermoula into the ghee. Add the prunes and if using dried figs add them at this stage. Pour in 300 ml water and put the lamb back into the tagine. Cover with the lid and put the tagine in the oven for about 2 hours.

Towards the end of the cooking time, melt the butter in a heavy-based pan, toss in the quinces and sauté until golden brown. Remove the tagine from the oven and place the golden quince around the meat (if using fresh figs, add them at this stage). Splash the orange flower water over the lamb and drizzle the honey over the meat and the fruit. Return the tagine to the oven for a further 25–30 minutes, until the meat and fruit are nicely browned and the lamb is so tender it almost falls off the bone. Sprinkle the chopped parsley and coriander over the top and serve immediately.

Earthy and fruity, with a hint of ginger, this tagine is a good winter warmer. It can be made with either fresh or pre-cooked beetroot. You could also serve roasted pumpkin or butternut squash and couscous (see page 60) tossed with pistachios or pine nuts.

1–2 tablespoons ghee (see page 9)
3–4 garlic cloves, crushed
1 red onion, halved lengthways and sliced with the grain
40 g fresh ginger, peeled and finely chopped or grated
1 red chilli, deseeded and sliced
2 teaspoons coriander seeds, crushed
2 cinnamon sticks
3–4 beetroots, peeled and quartered
500 g lean beef, cut into bite-sized cubes or strips
2 thin-skinned oranges, cut into segments
1 tablespoon dark, runny honey
1–2 tablespoons orange flower water
sea salt and freshly ground black pepper
a knob of butter
2–3 tablespoons shelled pistachio nuts
a small bunch of fresh flat leaf parsley, roughly chopped

SERVES 4–6

beef tagine with beetroot and oranges

Melt the ghee in a tagine or heavy-based casserole, and stir in the garlic, onion and ginger until they begin to colour. Add the chilli, coriander seeds and cinnamon sticks. Add the beetroot and sauté for 2–3 minutes. Toss in the beef and sauté for 1 minute. Pour in enough water to almost cover the beef and beetroot and bring it to the boil. Reduce the heat, cover with a lid and simmer for 1 hour, until the meat is very tender.

Add the orange segments, honey and orange flower water to the tagine and season the dish with salt and pepper to taste. Cover with the lid and cook for a further 10–15 minutes.

Melt the butter in a small saucepan and toss in the pistachio nuts, stirring them over medium heat until they turn golden brown. Sprinkle them over the tagine along with the flat leaf parsley and serve.

This fairly fiery dish is laced with the powerful flavours and aromas of ras-el-hanout (see page 9), a traditional spice mix. Regional variations use turnip, yam, pumpkin or butternut squash instead of sweet potatoes. The tagine is best served with plain couscous (see page 60) or chunks of bread and cooling yoghurt or a glass of mint tea.

beef tagine with sweet potatoes, peas, ginger and ras-el-hanout

2 tablespoons ghee (see page 9), or olive oil

40 g fresh ginger, peeled and finely shredded

1 onion, finely chopped

1 kg lean beef, cubed

1–2 teaspoons ras-el-hanout (see page 9)

2 medium sweet potatoes, peeled and cubed

sea salt and freshly ground black pepper

500 g shelled fresh peas or frozen peas

2–3 tomatoes, skinned, deseeded and chopped

1 preserved lemon (see page 8), finely shredded or chopped

a small bunch of fresh coriander leaves, finely chopped

SERVES 4

Heat the ghee in a tagine or heavy-based casserole. Stir in the ginger and onion and sauté until soft. Toss in the beef and sear it on all sides, then stir in the ras-el-hanout. Pour in enough water to just cover the meat mixture and bring it to the boil. Reduce the heat, cover with the lid and cook gently for about 40 minutes.

Add the sweet potato to the tagine, season with salt and pepper to taste, cover with the lid and cook gently for a further 20 minutes, until the meat is tender. Toss in the peas and tomatoes, cover with the lid and cook for 5–10 minutes.

Sprinkle the preserved lemon and the coriander over the top and serve.

Variations of this great street dish can be found throughout the Maghreb. It is also often prepared as a snack in the home. In many households, kefta (poached meatballs) are prepared in batches and stored in the refrigerator. Kefta are usually quite fiery, so serve them with bread, parsley and yoghurt to temper their hotness.

kefta tagine with eggs and roasted cumin

FOR THE KEFTA:
225 g minced lamb
1 onion, finely chopped
1 teaspoon dried mint
1–2 teaspoons ras-el-hanout (see page 9)
½ teaspoon cayenne
a small bunch of fresh flat leaf parsley, finely chopped
sea salt and freshly ground black pepper

1 tablespoon butter
¼-½ teaspoon salt
1 teaspoon cayenne pepper or chopped dried chillies
4 medium or large eggs
1–2 teaspoons cumin seeds, dry-roasted and ground
a small bunch of fresh flat leaf parsley, roughly chopped

SERVES 4

To make the kefta, put the minced meat, onion, mint, ras-el-hanout, cayenne and parsley in a bowl, season to taste with salt and pepper and mix well together. Using your hands, knead the mixture and mould it into small balls, roughly the size of a quail's egg, so that you end up with about 12 balls.

Fill a tagine or casserole with water and bring it to the boil. Carefully drop in the kefta, a few at a time, and poach them for about 10 minutes, turning them so that they are cooked on all sides. Remove them with a slotted spoon and drain on kitchen paper. Reserve roughly 300 ml of the cooking liquid. (If not using the kefta immediately, transfer them to a plate to cool and store in the refrigerator for 2–3 days.)

Add the butter to the reserved cooking liquid in the tagine and bring the mixture to the boil. Stir in the salt and cayenne and drop in the poached kefta. Cook over high heat until almost all the liquid has evaporated. Carefully crack the eggs around the kefta, cover the tagine with a lid and leave the eggs to cook in the sauce and steam until they are just set. Sprinkle the roasted cumin and chopped parsley over the top of the dish. Serve immediately.

Tagines made with meatballs (kefta) do not require long cooking times. Generally, the sauce is prepared first and the meatballs are poached in it, until just cooked. This popular meatball recipe is quite light and lemony and is delicious served with a leafy salad and couscous (see page 60) tossed with chilli and herbs.

tagine of spicy kefta with lemon

FOR THE KEFTA:
450 g finely minced beef or lamb
1 onion, finely chopped or grated
a small bunch of fresh flat leaf parsley, finely chopped
1–2 teaspoons ground cinnamon
1 teaspoon ground cumin
1 teaspoon ground coriander
½ teaspoon cayenne pepper, or 1 teaspoon paprika
sea salt and freshly ground black pepper

1 tablespoon olive oil
1 tablespoon butter or ghee (see page 9)
1 onion, roughly chopped
2–3 garlic cloves, halved and crushed
a thumb-sized piece of fresh ginger, peeled and finely chopped
1 red chilli, thinly sliced
2 teaspoons ground turmeric
a small bunch of fresh coriander, roughly chopped
a small bunch of fresh mint leaves, chopped
freshly squeezed juice of 1 lemon
1 lemon, cut into 4 or 6 segments, with pips removed

SERVES 4–6

To make the kefta, pound the minced meat with your knuckles in a bowl. Using your hands, lift up the lump of minced meat and slap it back down into the bowl. Add the onion, parsley, cinnamon, cumin, coriander and cayenne, and season to taste with salt and black pepper. Using your hands, mix the ingredients together and knead well, pounding the mixture for a few minutes. Take pieces of the mixture and shape them into little walnut-sized balls, so that you end up with about 16 kefta. (These can be made ahead of time and kept in the refrigerator for 2–3 days.)

Heat the oil and butter together in a tagine or heavy-based casserole. Stir in the onion, garlic, ginger and chilli and sauté until they begin to brown. Add the turmeric and half the coriander and mint, and pour in roughly 300 ml water. Bring the water to the boil, reduce the heat and simmer, covered, for 10 minutes. Carefully place the kefta in the liquid, cover and poach the kefta for about 15 minutes, rolling them in the liquid from time to time so they are cooked well on all sides. Pour over the lemon juice, season the liquid with salt and tuck the lemon segments around the kefta. Poach for a further 10 minutes.

Sprinkle with the remaining coriander and mint and serve hot.

This is a classic, Spanish-influenced peasant dish, which is often eaten on its own with yoghurt and bread but is also served with grilled or roasted meats, such as lamb chops. Either chorizo or merguez sausages can be used, as both impart their spicy flavours to the dish. For a meatless version, just omit the sausage, as the chickpeas are extremely tasty on their own.

chickpea and chorizo tagine
with bay leaves, paprika and sage

175 g dried chickpeas, soaked overnight
   in plenty of water
2–3 tablespoons olive oil
2 red onions, cut in half lengthways,
   halved crossways, and sliced with
   the grain
2 garlic cloves, chopped
1 thin chorizo, roughly 15 cm long,
   sliced on the diagonal
2–3 fresh bay leaves
several sprigs of fresh thyme
1–2 teaspoons Spanish smoked paprika
a bunch of fresh sage leaves, shredded
freshly squeezed juice of 1 lemon
sea salt and freshly ground black pepper

SERVES 4

Drain the chickpeas, put them in a large saucepan and cover with plenty of water. Bring the water to the boil, reduce the heat and simmer for roughly 45 minutes or until the chickpeas are soft but still have a bite to them. Drain them and refresh under cold running water. Remove any loose skins.

Heat the olive oil in a tagine or heavy-based casserole. Stir in the onions and garlic and sauté until they begin to colour. Add the chorizo, bay leaves and thyme and sauté until lightly browned. Toss in the chickpeas, add the paprika and cover with a lid. Cook gently for 10–15 minutes, to allow the flavours to mingle.

Toss in the sage leaves and lemon juice. Season with salt and pepper to taste and serve hot with yoghurt or flat bread.

Preserved lemon (see page 8) and cracked green olives are two of the principal ingredients of traditional Moroccan cooking. You can buy the olives at Middle Eastern and North African stores and some delicatessens. The tagine can be made with chicken joints or a whole chicken. Serve with couscous (see page 60) and salad or vegetables such as steamed carrots tossed with spices and mint.

chicken tagine with preserved lemon, green olives and thyme

8–10 chicken thighs or 4 whole legs
1 tablespoon olive oil with a knob of butter
2 preserved lemons, cut into strips
175 g cracked green olives
1–2 teaspoons dried thyme or oregano

FOR THE MARINADE:
1 onion, grated
3 garlic cloves, crushed
25 g fresh ginger, peeled and grated
a small bunch of fresh coriander, finely chopped
a pinch of saffron threads
freshly squeezed juice of 1 lemon
1 teaspoon coarse sea salt
3–4 tablespoons olive oil
sea salt and freshly ground black pepper

SERVES 4

In a bowl, mix together all the ingredients for the marinade. Put the chicken thighs or legs in a shallow dish and coat them in the marinade, rubbing it into the skin. Cover and chill in the refrigerator for 1–2 hours.

Heat the olive oil with the butter in a tagine or heavy-based casserole. Remove the chicken pieces from the marinade and brown them in the oil. Pour over the marinade that is left in the dish and add enough water to come halfway up the sides of the chicken pieces. Bring the water to the boil, reduce the heat, cover with a lid and simmer for about 45 minutes, turning the chicken from time to time.

Add the preserved lemon, olives and half the thyme to the tagine. Cover again and simmer for a further 15–20 minutes. Check the seasoning and sprinkle the rest of the thyme over the top. Serve immediately from the tagine.

With the tangy notes of preserved lemon (see page 8) combined with the sweet grapes, this tagine is deliciously refreshing. It is best accompanied by buttery couscous (see page 60) or flatbread and a leafy salad. You can use ready-prepared artichoke hearts or bottoms, which are available frozen or tinned.

chicken tagine with harissa, artichokes and green grapes

4 chicken breasts, cut into thick strips or chunks
2 tablespoons olive oil
2 onions, halved lengthways and sliced with the grain
½ preserved lemon, thinly sliced
1–2 teaspoons sugar
1–2 teaspoons harissa paste (see page 9)
2 teaspoons tomato paste
300 ml chicken stock or water
1 x 390 g tin of artichoke hearts, drained, rinsed and halved
about 16 fresh green grapes, halved lengthways
a bunch of fresh coriander leaves, coarsely chopped
sea salt and freshly ground black pepper

FOR THE MARINADE:
2 garlic cloves, crushed
1 teaspoon ground turmeric
freshly squeezed juice of 1 lemon
1 tablespoon olive oil

SERVES 4

First, make the marinade. In a bowl, mix together the garlic, turmeric, lemon juice and olive oil. Toss the chicken in the mixture, then cover and leave in the refrigerator to marinate for 1–2 hours.

Heat the oil in a tagine or heavy-based casserole. Stir in the onions, preserved lemon and the sugar and sauté for 2–3 minutes, until slightly caramelized. Toss in the marinated chicken, then add the harissa and tomato pastes. Pour in the stock and bring it to the boil. Reduce the heat, cover with a lid, and cook gently for 15 minutes.

Toss in the artichoke hearts, cover with the lid again and cook for a further 5 minutes. Add the grapes with some of the coriander and season to taste with salt and pepper. Sprinkle with the remaining coriander to serve.

This tagine is both fruity and spicy, and the rosemary and ginger give it a delightful aroma. It can be made with chicken joints or pigeon breasts, pheasant or duck, and needs only a buttery couscous (see page 60) and a leafy salad to accompany it.

spicy chicken tagine with apricots, rosemary and ginger

2 tablespoons olive oil with a knob of butter
1 onion, finely chopped
3 sprigs of rosemary, 1 finely chopped, the other 2 cut in half
40 g fresh ginger, peeled and finely chopped
2 red chillies, deseeded and finely chopped
1–2 cinnamon sticks
8 chicken thighs
175 g ready-to-eat dried apricots
2 tablespoons clear honey
1 x 400 g tin of plum tomatoes with their juice
sea salt and freshly ground black pepper
a small bunch of fresh green or purple basil leaves

SERVES 4

Heat the oil and butter in a tagine or heavy-based casserole. Stir in the onion, chopped rosemary, ginger and chillies and sauté until the onion begins to soften. Stir in the halved rosemary sprigs and the cinnamon sticks. Add the chicken thighs and brown them on both sides. Toss in the apricots with the honey, then stir in the plum tomatoes with their juice. (Add a little water if necessary, to ensure there is enough liquid to cover the base of the tagine and submerge the apricots.) Bring the liquid to the boil, then reduce the heat. Cover with a lid and cook gently for 35–40 minutes.

Season to taste with salt and pepper. Shred the larger basil leaves and leave the small ones intact. Sprinkle them over the chicken and serve the dish immediately.

This traditional Moorish dish appears in various guises throughout the Arab-influenced world. Poultry cooked with dates and honey is probably one of the most ancient culinary combinations and the finished dish is deliciously succulent. You can substitute the duck with chicken, pigeon or poussins, if you prefer.

tagine of duck breasts with dates, honey and orange flower water

25 g fresh ginger, peeled and chopped
2–3 garlic cloves, chopped
2–3 tablespoons olive oil with a knob of butter
2 cinnamon sticks
4 duck breasts on the bone
2–3 tablespoons clear honey
225 g moist, stoned dates
1–2 tablespoons orange flower water
sea salt and freshly ground black pepper

TO SERVE:
1 tablespoon butter
2–3 tablespoons blanched almonds

SERVES 4

Using a mortar and pestle, pound the ginger and garlic to a paste. Heat the olive oil and butter in a tagine or heavy-based casserole, then stir in the ginger-garlic paste and the cinnamon sticks. Once the mixture begins to colour, add the duck breasts and brown the skin.

Stir in the honey and tuck the dates around the duck. Add enough water (the amount will vary according to the size of your tagine) to cover the base of the tagine and to come about one-third of the way up the duck breasts. Bring the water to the boil, reduce the heat and cover with a lid. Cook gently for about 25 minutes.

Add the orange flower water and season to taste with salt and pepper. Cover and cook for a further 5 minutes, or until the duck is tender.

In a frying pan, melt the butter and stir in the almonds. Sauté until golden brown and then scatter them over the duck. Serve immediately with a mound of couscous (see page 60), flavoured with lemon and herbs.

Baking whole fish in a tagine keeps the flesh deliciously moist. Obviously, you need to select fish that fits snugly into your tagine. The most popular fish for oven-baking in North Africa include red mullet, sardines, red snapper, grouper and sea bass. You could serve this dish with couscous (see page 60) or a tangy salad.

oven-baked tagine of red mullet, tomatoes and lime

2 tablespoons olive oil
25 g butter
2–3 garlic cloves, thinly sliced
3–4 good-sized red mullet, gutted and cleaned
sea salt
2–3 large tomatoes, thinly sliced
1 lime, thinly sliced

TO SERVE:
a small bunch of fresh flat leaf parsley, coarsely chopped
1 lime, cut into wedges

SERVES 3–4

Preheat the oven to 180°C (350°F) Gas 4.

Heat the olive oil and butter in a tagine or oven-proof dish. Stir in the garlic and sauté until it begins to brown. Put the fish in the tagine and cook it until the skin has browned and lightly buckled. (If you are using an oven-proof dish, you can brown the garlic and fish in a frying pan first.) Turn off the heat, sprinkle a little salt over the fish and tuck the slices of tomato and lime over and around them. Cover with the lid and cook in the oven for about 15 minutes.

Remove the lid and bake for a further 5–10 minutes, until the fish is cooked and nicely browned on top (you could do this under the grill, if you prefer).

Sprinkle the parsley over the top and serve with wedges of lime to squeeze over the fish.

The fish tagines of coastal Morocco are often made with whole fish, or with large chunks of fleshy fish such as sea bass, monkfish and cod. The fish is first marinated in the classic chermoula flavouring, and the dish is given an additional fillip with a little white wine or sherry. Serve with new potatoes and a leafy salad.

fish tagine with preserved lemon and mint

900 g fresh fish fillets, such as cod or haddock, cut into large chunks

2–3 tablespoons olive oil

1 red onion, finely chopped

2 carrots, finely chopped

2 celery sticks, finely chopped

1 preserved lemon (see page 8), finely chopped

1 x 400 g tin of plum tomatoes with their juice

150 ml fish stock or water

150 ml white wine or fino sherry

sea salt and freshly ground black pepper

a bunch of fresh mint leaves, finely shredded

FOR THE CHERMOULA:

2–3 garlic cloves, chopped

1 red chilli, deseeded and chopped

1 teaspoon sea salt

a small bunch of fresh coriander

a pinch of saffron threads

1–2 teaspoons ground cumin

3–4 tablespoons olive oil

freshly squeezed juice of 1 lemon

SERVES 4–6

First, make the chermoula. Using a mortar and pestle, pound the garlic and chilli with the salt to form a paste. Add the coriander leaves and pound to a coarse paste. Beat in the saffron threads and cumin and bind well with the olive oil and lemon juice (you can whizz all the ingredients together in an electric blender, if you prefer). Reserve 2 teaspoons of the mixture for cooking. Toss the fish chunks in the remaining chermoula, cover and leave to marinate in the refrigerator for 1–2 hours.

Heat the oil in a tagine or heavy-based casserole. Stir in the onion, carrots and celery and sauté until softened. Add the preserved lemon (reserving a little for sprinkling) with the reserved 2 teaspoons of chermoula and the tomatoes and stir in well. Cook gently for about 10 minutes to reduce the liquid, then add the stock and the wine or sherry. Bring the liquid to the boil, cover the tagine, reduce the heat and simmer for 10–15 minutes.

Toss the fish in the tagine, cover and cook gently for 6–8 minutes, until the fish is cooked through. Season to taste with salt and pepper, sprinkle with the reserved preserved lemon and the shredded mint leaves and serve immediately.

For this lovely tagine, flavoured with garlic, chilli, cumin and coriander (a popular version of Morocco's favourite chermoula spice mix), you can used any meaty white fish. Serve it as a meal in itself with chunks of fresh, crusty bread to mop up the delicious juices, or with a buttery couscous (see page 60).

tagine of monkfish, potatoes, cherry tomatoes and black olives

about 900 g monkfish tail, cut
    into chunks
about 12 small new potatoes
3 tablespoons olive oil with a knob
    of butter
3–4 garlic cloves, thinly sliced
12–16 cherry tomatoes
2 green peppers, grilled until black,
    skinned and cut into strips
sea salt and freshly ground black pepper
about 12 fleshy black olives
1 lemon, cut into wedges, to serve

FOR THE CHERMOULA:
2 garlic cloves
1 teaspoon coarse salt
1–2 teaspoons cumin seeds, crushed
    or ground
1 red chilli, deseeded and chopped
freshly squeezed juice of 1 lemon
2 tablespoons olive oil
a small bunch of fresh coriander,
    roughly chopped

SERVES 4–6

First, make the chermoula. Using a mortar and pestle, pound the garlic with the salt to a smooth paste. Add the cumin, chilli, lemon juice and olive oil and stir in the coriander. Put the fish in a shallow dish and rub it with most of the chermoula (reserve a little for cooking). Cover and leave to marinate in the refrigerator for 1–2 hours.

Meanwhile, bring a saucepan of water to the boil and drop in the potatoes. Boil vigorously for about 8 minutes to soften them a little, then drain and refresh under cold running water. Peel and cut them in half lengthways.

Heat 2 tablespoons olive oil with the butter in a tagine or heavy-based saucepan. Stir in the garlic and, when it begins to brown, add the tomatoes to soften them. Add the skinned peppers and the reserved chermoula, and season to taste with salt and pepper. Tip the mixture onto a plate.

Arrange the potatoes over the base of the tagine and spoon half of the tomato and pepper mixture over them. Place the chunks of marinated fish on top and spoon the rest of the tomato and pepper mixture over the fish. Tuck the olives in and around the fish and drizzle the remaining tablespoon of olive oil over the top. Pour in roughly 125 ml of water and check the seasoning. Cover with a lid and steam for 15–20 minutes, until the fish is cooked through. Serve immediately with wedges of lemon.

In some coastal areas of Morocco, such as Casablanca and Tangier, restaurants offer shellfish tagines – a modern speciality, rather than a traditional one. Whether these dishes are the result of colonial French influence or simply devised for the tourists, they are certainly very tasty. They are best appreciated on their own, with chunks of crusty bread to mop up the creamy sauce.

creamy shellfish tagine with fennel and harissa

500 g fresh mussels in their shells, scrubbed clean and rinsed
500 g fresh prawns in their shells, thoroughly rinsed
freshly squeezed juice of 1 lemon
2 tablespoons olive oil
4–6 shallots, finely chopped
1 fennel bulb, chopped
1–2 teaspoons harissa paste (see page 9)
150 ml double cream
sea salt and freshly ground black pepper
a generous bunch of fresh coriander, finely chopped

SERVES 4–6

Put the mussels and prawns in a wide saucepan with just enough water to cover them. Add the lemon juice, cover the pan and bring the liquid to the boil. Shake the pan and cook the shellfish for about 3 minutes, until the shells of the mussels have opened. Drain the shellfish, reserve the liquor, and discard any mussels that have not opened. Refresh the mussels and prawns under cold running water and shell most of them (you can, of course, leave them all in their shells if you prefer, as long as you are prepared for messy eating).

Heat the olive oil in a tagine or heavy-based casserole. Stir in the shallots and fennel and sauté until soft. Stir in the harissa and pour in 300 ml of the reserved cooking liquor. Bring the liquid to the boil and continue to boil for 2–3 minutes, reduce the heat and stir in the cream. Simmer gently for about 5 minutes to let the flavours mingle, season to taste with salt and lots of black pepper, and stir in the mussels and prawns. Toss in half the coriander, cover with a lid and cook gently for about 5 minutes. Sprinkle the remaining coriander over the top and serve immediately.

Substantial enough for a main meal, served with couscous (see page 60) and yoghurt, vegetable tagines also make good side dishes for grilled or roasted meats or other tagines. You can cook this one in the oven if you like, using the tagine base or an oven-proof pan.

tagine of butternut squash, shallots, sultanas and almonds

3 tablespoons olive oil with a knob of butter

about 12 pink shallots, peeled and left whole

about 8 garlic cloves, lightly crushed

120 g sultanas

120 g blanched almonds

1–2 teaspoons harissa paste (see page 9)

2 tablespoons dark, runny honey

1 medium butternut squash, halved lengthways, peeled, deseeded and sliced

sea salt and freshly ground black pepper

a small bunch of fresh coriander leaves, finely chopped

1 lemon, cut into quarters, to serve

SERVES 3–4

Heat the oil and butter in a tagine or heavy-based casserole. Stir in the shallots and garlic and sauté them until they begin to colour. Add the sultanas and almonds and stir in the harissa and honey. Toss in the squash, making sure it is coated in the spicy oil. Pour in enough water to cover the base of the tagine and cover with the lid. Cook gently for 15–20 minutes, until the shallots and squash are tender but still quite firm.

Season to taste with salt and pepper, sprinkle the coriander leaves over the top and serve with wedges of lemon to squeeze over the dish.

You can make this hearty country dish with either fresh or frozen artichokes. If using fresh, you must first remove the outer leaves, then cut off the stems and scoop out the choke and hairy bits with a teaspoon. Rub the artichokes with lemon juice or place in a bowl of cold water with lemon juice to prevent discoloration.

tagine of artichokes, potatoes, peas and saffron

2–3 tablespoons olive oil
2 red onions, halved lengthways, cut in half crossways, and sliced with the grain
4 garlic cloves, crushed
2 teaspoons coriander seeds
1 teaspoon cumin seeds
2 teaspoons ground turmeric
1–2 teaspoons dried mint
8 medium waxy potatoes, peeled and quartered
350 ml vegetable or chicken stock
4 prepared artichokes, quartered
a small bunch of fresh coriander leaves, chopped
225 g shelled fresh peas or frozen peas
½ preserved lemon (see page 8), finely shredded
sea salt and freshly ground black pepper
a small bunch of fresh mint leaves, to serve

SERVES 4–6

Heat the olive oil in a tagine or heavy-based casserole, add the onion and sauté until it begins to soften. Add the garlic, coriander and cumin seeds, ground turmeric and the dried mint. Toss in the potatoes, coating them in the spices. Pour in the stock and bring it to the boil. Reduce the heat, cover with a lid and cook gently for about 10 minutes.

Toss in the artichokes and fresh coriander and cook for a further 5 minutes. Stir in the peas and preserved lemon, and season to taste with salt and pepper. Cook gently for 5–10 minutes, uncovered, until the artichokes are tender and the liquid has reduced.

Sprinkle with the fresh mint leaves and serve with couscous (see page 60) or chunks of fresh, crusty bread.

This syrupy, caramelized tagine is delicious served as a main dish, with couscous (see page 60) and a herby salad, or as a side dish to accompany grilled or roasted meats. Sweet potatoes, butternut squash and pumpkin can be used instead of yam, if you prefer.

tagine of yam, shallots, carrots and prunes

2–3 tablespoons olive oil with a knob of butter
40 g fresh ginger, peeled and finely chopped or grated
1–2 cinnamon sticks or 1–2 teaspoons ground cinnamon
about 16 small shallots, peeled and left whole
700 g yam, peeled and cut into bite-sized chunks
2 medium carrots, peeled and cut into bite-sized chunks
175 g ready-to-eat, stoned prunes
1 tablespoon dark, runny honey
425 ml vegetable or chicken stock
a small bunch of fresh coriander leaves, roughly chopped
a few fresh mint leaves, chopped
sea salt and freshly ground black pepper

SERVES 4–6

Heat the olive oil and butter in a tagine or heavy-based casserole, and stir in the ginger and cinnamon sticks. Toss in the shallots and when they begin to colour add the yam and the carrots. Sauté for 2–3 minutes, then add the prunes and the honey. Pour in the stock and bring it to the boil. Reduce the heat, cover with a lid and cook gently for about 25 minutes.

Remove the lid and stir in some of the coriander and mint. Season to taste with salt and pepper and reduce the liquid, if necessary, by cooking for a further 2–3 minutes without the lid. The vegetables should be tender and slightly caramelized in a very syrupy sauce. Sprinkle with the remaining coriander and mint and serve immediately.

As butter beans are so meaty, this tagine can be served as a main dish, but it is also excellent as an accompaniment to grilled or roasted meats and poultry. Bean dishes like this vary from region to region in Morocco, sometimes spiked with chillies or hot chorizo-style sausages.

tagine of butter beans, cherry tomatoes and black olives

175 g dried butter beans, soaked overnight in plenty of water

2–3 tablespoons olive oil with a knob of butter

4 garlic cloves, halved and crushed

2 red onions, halved lengthways, cut in half crossways, and sliced with the grain

1–2 red or green chillies, deseeded and thinly sliced

1–2 teaspoons coriander seeds, crushed

25 g fresh ginger, peeled and finely shredded or chopped

a pinch of saffron threads

about 16–20 cherry tomatoes

1–2 teaspoons granulated sugar

1–2 teaspoons dried thyme

2–3 tablespoons black olives, stoned

freshly squeezed juice of 1 lemon

sea salt and freshly ground black pepper

a small bunch of flat leaf parsley, coarsely chopped

SERVES 4–6

Drain and rinse the soaked beans. Put them in a deep saucepan with plenty of water and bring to the boil. Boil for about 5 minutes, then reduce the heat and simmer gently for about 1 hour, or until the beans are tender but not mushy. Drain and refresh them under cold running water.

Heat the olive oil and butter in a tagine or heavy-based casserole. Stir in the garlic, onions and chillies and sauté until they soften. Add the coriander seeds, ginger and saffron. Cover and cook gently for 4–5 minutes. Toss in the tomatoes with the sugar and thyme, cover with the lid again, and cook until the skin on the tomatoes begins to crinkle.

Toss in the beans and olives, pour over the lemon juice and season to taste with salt and pepper. Cover with the lid and cook gently for about 5 minutes, until the beans and olives are heated through. Sprinkle with the flat leaf parsley and serve with chunks of crusty bread and a dollop of thick, creamy yoghurt, if liked.

This vegetarian tagine is best made with baby aubergines, but you can also use slender, larger aubergines cut into quarters lengthways. As a main dish, it is delicious served with couscous (see page 60), or bulghur, and a dollop of thick, creamy yoghurt; it can also be served as a side dish to accompany meat or poultry.

tagine of baby aubergines
with coriander and mint

1–2 tablespoons olive oil

1 tablespoon butter or ghee (see page 9)

1–2 red onions, halved lengthways and sliced with the grain

3–4 garlic cloves, crushed

1–2 red chillies, deseeded and sliced, or 2–3 dried red chillies, left whole

1–2 teaspoons coriander seeds, roasted and crushed

1–2 teaspoons cumin seeds, roasted and crushed

2 teaspoons granulated sugar

16 baby aubergines, with stalks intact

2 x 400 g tins of chopped tomatoes

sea salt and freshly ground black pepper

a bunch of fresh mint leaves, roughly chopped

a bunch of fresh coriander, roughly chopped

SERVES 4

Heat the oil and butter in a tagine or heavy-based casserole. Stir in the onions and garlic and sauté until they begin to colour. Add the chillies, the coriander and cumin seeds and the sugar. When the seeds give off a nutty aroma, toss in the whole baby aubergines, coating them in the onion and spices. Tip in the tomatoes, cover with a lid and cook gently for about 40 minutes, until the aubergines are beautifully tender.

Season to taste with salt and pepper and add half the mint and coriander leaves. Cover and simmer for a further 5–10 minutes. Sprinkle with the remaining mint and coriander leaves and serve hot.

This country-style dish is vegetarian, typical of regions where meat is regarded as a luxury by most families. Pulses of all kinds and, in particular, chickpeas, provide the nourishing content of these dishes. To avoid lengthy preparation and cooking, use tinned chickpeas. For simple accompaniments, offer yoghurt or bread.

spicy carrot and chickpea tagine with turmeric and coriander

3–4 tablespoons olive oil
1 onion, finely chopped
3–4 garlic cloves, finely chopped
2 teaspoons ground turmeric
1–2 teaspoons cumin seeds
1 teaspoon ground cinnamon
½ teaspoon cayenne pepper
½ teaspoon ground black pepper
1 tablespoon dark, runny honey
3–4 medium carrots, sliced on
    the diagonal
2 x 410 g tins of chickpeas, thoroughly
    rinsed and drained
sea salt
1–2 tablespoons rosewater
a bunch of fresh coriander leaves,
    finely chopped
1 lemon, cut into wedges, to serve

SERVES 4

Heat the oil in a tagine or heavy-based casserole, add the onion and garlic and sauté until soft. Add the turmeric, cumin, cinnamon, cayenne, black pepper, honey and carrots. Pour in enough water to cover the base of the tagine and cover with a lid. Cook gently for 10–15 minutes.

Toss in the chickpeas, check that there is still enough liquid at the base of the tagine, cover with the lid, and cook gently for a further 5–10 minutes. Season with salt, sprinkle the rosewater and coriander leaves over the top and serve with lemon wedges.

ACCOMPANIMENTS

plain buttery couscous

350 g couscous, rinsed and drained
½ teaspoon sea salt
400 ml warm water
2 tablespoons sunflower or olive oil
25 g butter, broken into little pieces

SERVES 4

Couscous is the staple grain of the Maghreb. It is generally made from semolina, but can also be made from barley and maize. Couscous can be served plain or with herbs, spices, nuts or fruits. For a fiery taste, the grains are rubbed with harissa (see page 9).

Preheat the oven to 180°C (350°F) Gas 4.

Tip the couscous into an oven-proof dish. Stir the salt into the water and pour it over the couscous. Leave the couscous to absorb the water for about 10 minutes.

Using your fingers, rub the oil into the grains to break up the lumps and air them. Dot the butter over the surface and cover with a piece of foil or wet greaseproof paper. Put the dish in the oven for about 15 minutes to heat through.

Fluff up the grains with a fork and serve the couscous from the dish, or tip it onto a plate piled high in a pyramid.

Note: 500 g couscous made with wheat or maize flours serves about 6 people. You need approximately the following proportions of salted water to couscous: 500 g barley couscous needs soaking in 500 ml water; 500 g seffa (ultrafine) couscous needs 600 ml water.

orange salad with red onions and black olives

3 fresh oranges, peeled with a knife to remove the pith, and thinly sliced
1 red onion, thinly sliced into rings
about 12 black olives, stoned
2–3 tablespoons olive oil
freshly squeezed juice of 1 lime
sea salt
1 teaspoon cumin seeds, roasted
½ teaspoon smoked paprika
a small bunch of fresh coriander leaves, coarsely chopped

SERVES 4

Juicy salads made with citrus fruits, such as oranges and grapefruits, are popular accompaniments to the spicier, and sometimes fiery, tagines. Colourful and refreshing, this salad is also delicious with grilled and roasted meats.

Arrange the orange slices on a serving dish or in a shallow bowl and place the onion slices and olives on top.

In a small bowl, mix together the olive oil, lime juice and salt to taste and pour the dressing over the oranges. Sprinkle the cumin seeds, paprika and coriander leaves over the top and serve.

country salad with peppers and chillies

Fresh country salads vary according to the season but generally they are crunchy and tangy, and often packed with fresh herbs to cleanse the palate. A salad may be offered at the start of the meal to whet the appetite, or as an accompaniment to the heavier, syrupy tagines to cut the sweetness.

2 red onions, finely chopped
1 red pepper, deseeded and chopped
1 green pepper, deseeded and chopped
2 green chillies, deseeded and chopped
2 celery sticks, chopped
2 garlic cloves, chopped
a generous bunch of fresh mint leaves, chopped
a generous bunch of fresh flat leaf parsley, chopped
2 tablespoons olive oil
freshly squeezed juice of ½ lemon
sea salt and freshly ground black pepper

SERVES 4

In a bowl, mix together the chopped onions, peppers, chillies, celery, garlic, mint and parsley. Add the olive oil, lemon juice and salt and pepper to taste. Toss the salad thoroughly and serve.

melon and mint salad with orange flower water

This refreshing salad is an ideal accompaniment to spicy tagines. It is also served as a palate cleanser between the richly flavoured tagine and the ensuing course of plain or lightly flavoured couscous.

1 ripe honeydew or galia melon, deseeded and cut into bite-sized chunks

a bunch of fresh mint leaves, finely shredded (reserve a few leaves for garnishing)

2 tablespoons orange flower water

1 tablespoon sugar or clear honey (optional)

SERVES 4

In a bowl, toss the melon chunks with the mint and orange flower water, and sugar or honey, if using. Cover and chill in the refrigerator for 1–2 hours. Sprinkle with a few mint leaves and serve.

index